C000246969

STRENGTH

for the

SOUL

BY ERIC SANDOR

Published by Pinpoint Media 2020

The right of Eric Sandor to be identified as the Author of the Work has been asserted by him
in accordance with the Copyright, Designs and Patents Act 1988.

Cover design by Joseph Paul
www.josephpaul.co.uk

ISBN: 978-1-8383352-0-5 Hardback

IN LOVING MEMORY OF TY PAGE
30TH MAY 1958 – 1ST JUNE 2017

You are the most joy-filled, giant-hearted worshipper, and greatest
friend I have known. You were a blessing to so many, and still are,
even in your absence.

FOR MY CHILDREN
SAMUEL, COLUMBUS, LILY & GISELE

AND FOR MY GODCHILDREN
ELIAS, CHRISTIAN, STEPHEN, CORDELIA & LEVI

May you always find hope, joy and assurance in the all-conquering
love of God and know His great affection for you.

FOREWORD FROM THE AUTHOR

While beauty may be said to be skin-deep, true strength is soul-deep. We need strength in our inner beings to make the very most of life – particularly amidst pain, hardship, and temptation. Our souls are strengthened with nourishment and exercise. As we meditate on the truth, we feed our souls. And as we worship in contemplation of the beauty of God and the wonder of his ways, we build muscles in the depths of our being. This collection of prayers and meditations is intended to help you do just that – to build inner strength that will endure, by establishing greater intimacy with Jesus.

The conversations with God captured in these daily devotions are genuine experiences from my walk with Jesus and many are a pure record of my prayers and spontaneous praise for Him over recent months, through the enormous challenges of 2020. This year has been a time of loss and lament. God is stirring up his people to come to Him in complete honesty, and with a rawness of spirit that leads to repentance and renewal. God meets us where we are and trades his beauty for our ashes, hope for our despair, and healing for our brokenness. The key in this Holy exchange, is of course that we must do our part.

My prayer is that you might use some of my prayers and exclamations of praise in this book, as a jumping-off point for your own authentic conversations with Jesus, and that these may inspire you to offer Him a sacrifice of praise, whatever your circumstances may be. He is certainly worthy of all we could ever give Him, and more. My hope is that the Lord uses this book to draw you to a quiet place with Jesus, and that through that time, you enter into a more trusting, intimate relationship with Him. I pray that you encounter God within these writings and images and that you are strengthened a little by each one, as you wrestle with your faith, and as you stir up honest prayers and praise for our ever-loving, ever-faithful Heavenly Father.

UNITY

PROMISE FAVOURITE

FREEDOM   HOLY

SATISFACTION   HOPE

DELIGHT   FAITH

INTIMACY   SUFFERING

WORSHIP   PATIENCE

SACRIFICE   PERSEVERANCE

FORGIVENESS   INADEQUACY

TRUTH   POWER

JOY   DISCIPLINE

PEACE   VICTORY

TRUST   RECKLESS

PRAYER   ADVENTURE

DEVOTION   OFFERING

LOVE   PERMANENCE

LOVE

Love is patient, love is kind. It does not envy, it does not boast, it is not proud.
It does not dishonor others, it is not self-seeking, it is not easily angered, it keeps
no record of wrongs. Love does not delight in evil but rejoices with the truth.
It always protects, always trusts, always hopes, always perseveres. Love never fails.

1 CORINTHIANS 13:4-8A NIV

The sun rises over the hard land.

Cool light blankets the brittle grass and trees, reviving all it touches, bringing fresh hope for the new day.

The earth softens and all living things turn towards the sun's radiance for strength. A single life source sustaining all.

This is love. The most powerful force in the universe burns within the human chest and motivates us to action.

Like the sun, love gives and gives and gives but is never diminished. Love multiplies from soul to soul. Ever-expanding in influence and reach, love is eternal and is a glimpse of the divine.

Love revives the weary and comforts the broken. It emboldens the fainthearted.

Brings dreams to the heart of the pessimist. Invites the cynic on an adventure. Love penetrates the coldest, darkest places. It always finds a way, makes a way, and shows the way.

Everything in the world that has virtue, was born from love, and anything that is loveless is worthless. It is the only true measure of value and is our greatest aspiration.

Our life's purpose is to love and be loved. To shine like the sun. We were made for love.

God is love and the greatest expression of His love – the personification of His infinitely powerful, never-ending love – is His son, Jesus.

Will you join with all creation and turn your face towards the Son?

DEVOTION

My passion is to be consumed with Him... I continually long to know the wonders of Jesus more fully and to experience the overflowing power of his resurrection working in me. I will be one with him in his sufferings and I will be one with him in his death. Only then will I be able to experience complete oneness with him in his resurrection from the realm of death.

PHILIPPIANS 3:9-11 TPT

Love gives birth to longing, which grows into a hot burning desire.

A fiery passion that empowers us to withstand the fiercest storm. To scale the highest walls. To risk all that we have and even to sacrifice our very selves in pursuit of complete union with the object of our affection.

A love-union in which adoration is mutually reciprocated in equally unbounded measure.

Any thoughts of discretion or advice towards moderation are swiftly consumed in the fire that overwhelms our being; that demands our full attention; commandeers all our faculties and requires all our strength to be deployed in its expression.

When fully grown, this love union occupies all of our spirit, soul, and body. There is no room for any other motivating force. All our thoughts, dreams, words and actions are the product of love. A love that has been deeply felt, deeply held and passionately pursued dominates our being. And then love has become devotion.

Will you throw yourself into the all consuming fire of God's love, with no thought for tomorrow?

PRAYER

Sighing has become my daily food; my groans pour out like water.

JOB 3:24 NIV

Longing and yearning pool together in my soul.

They gather into a reservoir, pregnant with expectation and intent. They cry out to all the cells of my body, demanding to be manifested in the world. To find some realisation and fulfilment in physical form. To amount to something more than invisible emotion.

The urgency and legitimacy of their appeal is impossible to ignore. They dominate the airwaves of my mind, occupy the beat of my heart, and yet go unfulfilled. Without resolution. Throughout every wakeful hour, my ears are filled with their desperate, impassioned demand for justice. I am compelled to answer, but unable to form an adequate response. Unable to realise their ambition to force the world around me to conform to their groans.

And so the only consequence of their soundless, incessant outcry, is my tears. My heart and soul are hijacked and convulse with sobbing.

Longing and yearning flood my being.

My mouth gives voice to their wails. My eyes, at last, yield the precious product of their urgent appeal. The water of my tears. The ultimate physical manifestation of their burning desire.

In my inability and inadequacy, the sound and saltwater of my weeping become prayer. My contribution to resolving the brokenness around me joins with the water and wails of others around the world. They gather in the hands of the one who created the universe. They unite and accumulate in heaven. And one day the dam will burst.

One day our world will change and conform to the substance of our longings. Until then, longing and yearning call out to us in the streets and across the treetops.

Who will carry their cry?

TRUST

Trust in the Lord completely, and do not rely on your own opinions.
With all your heart rely on him to guide you, and he will lead you in every
decision you make. Become intimate with him in whatever you do,
and he will lead you wherever you go.

PROVERBS 3:5-6 TPT

I fall into His arms with complete dependence.

Surrendering any thought of remaining responsible for standing on my own two feet, I collapse all of my weight onto Him.

I rest there in His embrace. Laying motionless, draped across His lap. I have placed my being into His hands.

As He holds me, I make no effort. Not a single muscle in my being is exerted, as I relax into the reality of being carried. I simply breathe and feel the weight of every part of me, being held up and supported.

There is no part of my soul that now stands in its own strength. The weight of all my hopes and longings, all my challenges and burdens are now carried by another. I have no thoughts of insecurity, no concerns about what may become of me or my dreams.

His breath fills my lungs and sustains me. He carries me through each moment of the day and He carries me into the future. I have no worry about tomorrow.

He guides my thoughts, whispers wisdom in my ears and directs my path. He shows me the way through the darkest caverns. My whole being is attentive with expectation to find the way that He is making for me, because He always does and He always will. I know with all certainty that He is always clearing a path to goodness for me.

I have given Him my life. I trust in Him, and Him alone.

Where have you chosen to place your weight?

PEACE

---

*Lord, even when your path takes me through the valley of deepest darkness,
fear will never conquer me, for you already have! You remain close to me and
lead me through it all the way. Your authority is my strength and my peace.
The comfort of your love takes away my fear. I'll never be lonely, for you are near.*

PSALM 23:4 TPT

My heart sings to the Lord. There is no one like You! No one loves me like You do! No one else lifts my soul. You are the only one who saves and who turns things around. You are the only one who heals the broken-hearted and brings hope to the needy.

You make a way for me when there is none. You surround me with your love and defend me on every side.

You are watching over me and watching over all your promises to ensure they are fulfilled.

When I rise in the morning, You give me strength. When I lay down to sleep, You comfort me. You are with me constantly. You are in my every thought, guiding me, encouraging me, protecting me. There is nowhere I can go to stray from You, and nothing I can do to lose your affection, for You have found me and You will never let me go. You will be with me forever, and I will enjoy your goodness and mercy every day of my life.

I am yours, and You are mine.

Even when I fail, or fall down, or suffer loss. Even when my life and the lives of those I love, hover on a knife's edge, I am totally fearless. Whatever the circumstances – even when I am outnumbered, overpowered, and overwhelmed by a tidal wave of opposition, my spirit is stilled in the knowledge that You alone are God and You have adopted me as your son, whom You adore.

I am filled with boldness and courage, and won't be intimidated by anything, because You always have my back. Nothing can ever separate me from You. And if I always have You with me, what is there to be afraid of?

All my hope is in You. Your love never fails. And so, my soul is full of peace.

Where does your assurance come from?

JOY

Those who sow with tears will reap with songs of joy. Those who go out weeping, carrying seed to sow, will return with songs of joy, carrying sheaves with them.

PSALM 126:5-6 NIV

You turned my mourning into joy. I lost my beloved to cancer. The love of my youth and mother of my children was taken from us. My closest friend followed 6 months later.

The heart of my young daughter stopped and You revived her. You brought her back to me from the edge of darkness.

You heard all my cries. You collected all my tears, gathering and holding them like treasure. You held me all the while. You lift my chin and wipe my cheeks dry.

You smile at me, face to face. With tears in your eyes, You speak my name and call me your beloved son. And I feel the full force of your love. It warms the coldness in my soul. Your love reaches into me, to the places long neglected – softening the hard ground, bringing light to the darkest corners.

Your tenderness is a balm for my wounds and You pull me to my feet. With your arm around me, I take small, tentative, painful steps into the future. And we stayed together like that for more than three years, walking in-step slowly, while I limped and leaned on You. And then You invited me to run with You. You told me I was ready, and I believed You. So we did. We ran together with wind in our faces. I looked over at You running with me, smiling at me with pride. And to my surprise, I discovered a joy within.

You suggested that I could let go of the pain of the past and could receive new joy and newness of life. So I did. I opened all of my being to You, without reservation, and breathed out all the grief I had been holding onto.

You restored my soul with your love and faithfulness. As I breathed You in, You brought deep joy to a broken heart, and You healed me. My soul will rejoice in your goodness and mercy forever. My joy is found in being with You. In running with You.

Where does your joy come from?

TRUTH

Jesus said... "When you continue to embrace all that I teach, you prove that you are my true followers. For if you embrace the truth, it will release more freedom into your lives."

JOHN 8:31-32 TPT

It was the dead of night and a myriad of stars shone overhead. In one month we were to be married and I was wrestling with guilty secrets as I looked up to the sky.

I knelt down to pray. After some minutes, I found myself standing before the judgement seat of Jesus. His eyes burned right through me and I squirmed with anguish as I felt overcome with shame. The floor seemed to fall from beneath my feet. I had no arguments in my defence, nowhere to hide, and no basis on which to stand. It was excruciating.

I cried out in tears for Jesus to forgive me. To have mercy on me, and to save me from the filth that I now saw permeated my soul.

All at once, a peace came over me, together with a sense of great assurance. But I also received a command. I needed to confess my sins to my future wife and to ask for her forgiveness.

I did so, and a few bitterly painful days followed, until the moment my beloved looked in my eyes and told me she forgave me. I had never felt so loved. I had never felt so accepted. I realized that she truly loved me as I was. Prior to that moment, deep within, I had unknowingly discounted her love because I had been wearing a mask. Did she love me or the man I presented through the mask?

Hiding and keeping secrets is a burden that creates dark places in our lives. And this darkness steals and cheats us from the beautiful intimacy that is only felt in the light of genuine acceptance and love. Getting real with Jesus and those we love is the only way to an abundant life. The truth sets us free to love and be loved.

Are you hiding behind a mask?

Is it time for you to come out of your cave and get real with Jesus and your family?

FORGIVENESS

Be merciful, just as your Father is merciful. Do not judge, and you will not be judged. Do not condemn, and you will not be condemned. Forgive, and you will be forgiven. Give, and it will be given to you. A good measure, pressed down, shaken together and running over, will be poured into your lap. For with the measure you use, it will be measured to you.

LUKE 6:36-38 NIV

I was guilty and You set me free.

You paid my penalty and took my punishment. You gave me a clean slate. A fresh start. You let me off the hook, scot-free.

My guilt and shame were erased and I received a new lease of life. All I needed to do was to accept it, which I did with both hands. I grabbed hold of it in desperation and your forgiveness brought healing to my soul.

And then You showed me how outrageously unfair it was. How mercy and justice were opposites. How I wanted mercy for myself while desiring others to receive the punishment they deserved.

You showed me that the measure of mercy I used for others would determine the measure of mercy You gave me. My mercy or judgement towards others would be mirrored back to me. And this is the way the scales are balanced, and the way You can pour out mercy with fairness across all mankind. Each of us determines how much of your infinite mercy we are qualified to receive.

And so I released everyone from judgement and wanted everyone to receive this amazing grace. But still I found unforgiveness buried deep in my heart. You brought it to light. You helped me uproot it and throw it away. And that's when I discovered a whole new realm of freedom and wellbeing.

Yes, receiving forgiveness is medicine for the soul, but harbouring unforgiveness is a poison that disfigures and destroys.

Oh Lord, help me to show others the extravagant mercy that You have lavished on me.

Who do you need to forgive?

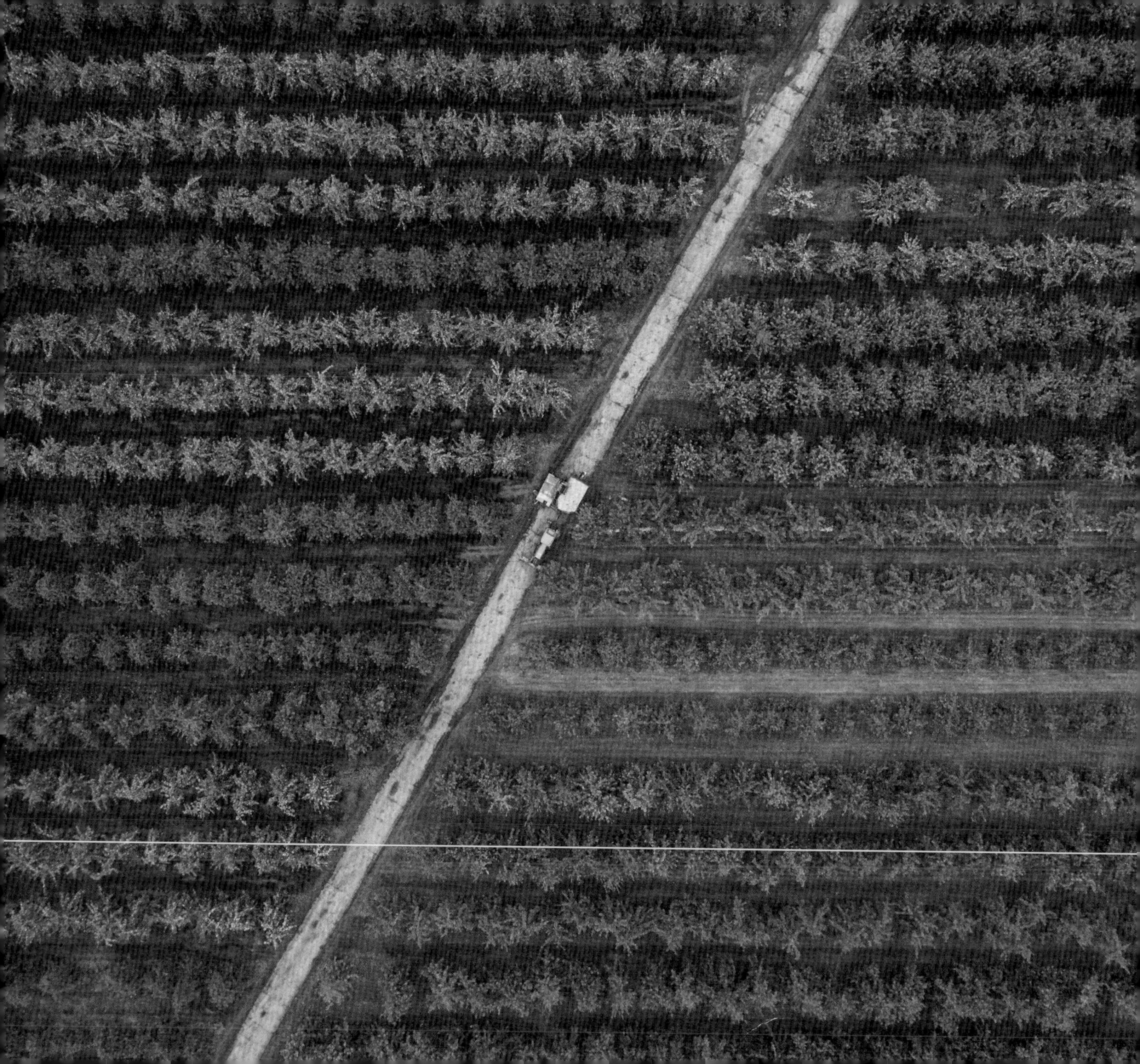

SACRIFICE

So we no longer offer up a steady stream of blood sacrifices, but through Jesus, we will offer up to God a steady stream of praise sacrifices – these are 'the lambs' we offer from our lips that celebrate his name! We will show mercy to the poor and not miss an opportunity to do acts of kindness for others, for these are the true sacrifices that delight God's heart.

HEBREWS 13:15-16 TPT

After World War II, the following prayer was found pinned to the clothes of a dead child at Ravensbruck concentration camp:

"O Lord, remember not only the men and women of good will, but also those of ill will. But do not remember all of the suffering they have inflicted upon us. Instead remember the fruits we have borne because of this suffering – our fellowship, our loyalty to one another, our humility, our courage, our generosity, the greatness of heart that has grown from this trouble. When our persecutors come to be judged by you, let all of these fruits that we have borne be their forgiveness."

This vast generosity of spirit is truly astonishing. To not only forgive your tormentors, but to go so far as to ask God to accept your suffering at their hands, as a sacrifice for their redemption?

The strength and compassion of this attitude is beyond comprehension. Yet, this is what Jesus did for all mankind and He calls us to walk the same road. To lay down our rights and turn the other cheek. To carry our cross.

As we become like Jesus, we are so full of God's love that no sacrifice is too large for us. In fact, we develop a deep sense that He is so worthy of all our adoration, that any sacrifice is seen as an opportunity to give Him worship. To offer Him something truly precious and to show Him our love. To praise Him even in disappointment, hardship and suffering. To be a champion for the oppressed and 'servant' of the poor.

Oh that we would all have the occasion in our lives to show our Heavenly Father just how much we love Him through a pure and true sacrifice and that we would give him the worship He deserves.

Have you been given an opportunity to offer God a sacrifice of praise?

WORSHIP

Oh, the depth of the riches of the wisdom and knowledge of God!
How unsearchable his judgments, and his paths beyond tracing out! Who has
known the mind of the Lord? Or who has been his counselor? Who has ever
given to God, that God should repay them? For from him and through him
and for him are all things. To him be the glory forever! Amen.

ROMANS 11:33-36 NIV

My soul magnifies the Lord. It brings Him into focus for all to see his majesty, his sovereignty, and his beauty. His ways are brought to light. His gentle and tender mercy. His compassion and faithfulness. His ways that lead us into the unknown on an adventure of faith and trust. His ways that empower all of creation with freedom. Freedom to choose, and freedom to write our own future. Yes, each one of us is free to love or to hate. To forgive or to hold in judgement. And in God's integrity, He honours our choices. Goes along with our desires. Listens to our prayers and actions them.

But in his great mercy, for all people who love Him – for those who know his ways and walk in them – He puts prayers in our souls. He places desires in our hearts and guides us down paths that lead to goodness. And all the while, He bulldozes a way ahead of us and his love is our forcefield. Our shield against evil on all sides. And so we walk with Him with hope and joy. With confidence in his desired future for us and those we love. Even in pain and loss we look forward to restoration and we trust in his unfailing love.

Yes, my soul magnifies the Lord. It shouts the truth of how He pursues every person with passion. How He saves to the outer edges of the universe. How He never gives up on us and He never fails to reach out with love to all of creation. My soul spreads his fame; desires all to know how incomparable He is; how completely unique He is across all galaxies and constellations. Yes, He is off the charts. He is uncontainable, indescribable, undefeatable, and inestimable. He is limitless in all his qualities and everything He does is an expression of 100% pure love. Because that is who He is. He is Love personified. Love unleashed and Love through and through. He is altogether trustworthy. Altogether faithful. Altogether worthy of all our praise and worship.

Yes, my soul magnifies the Lord, and He makes me sing with joy. He makes me shout to the skies and dance with delight. He makes me stomp my feet on the mountains of despair until they are molehills. Until they are dust beneath my feet. My soul magnifies the Lord until all my troubles are like grains of sand. He is my great defender. My friend. He is the lover of my soul and I will use all the freedom I possess to worship Him with my life forever.

What does your soul bring into focus? Does it make your heart sing and shout and dance?

INTIMACY

He is within me – I am his garden of delight.
I have him fully and now he fully has me!

SONG OF SONGS 6:3 TPT

Oh Lord You are the light within my hard centre. You fashion beauty from the rough edges of my heart. You are a craftsman working in the minute details of my soul; carving and shaping; polishing and shining; creating a diamond out of the pressure and suffering of life. Bringing colour and light to my cold darkness. Yes, You dwell and work across every inch of my very soul. Deep within me your light shines and ignites every fibre of my being, bringing beauty from the ashes of regret and sorrow.

You fill me with your life. You are my breath. You are the air in which I move, and live and have my being. You are all around me and You fill my lungs. You sustain my heartbeat. You are in my every thought. Whispering wisdom. Giving me intuition for each blind step I need to take. Your Spirit permeates every cell of my being and overflows in my thoughts, words, and actions.

Oh, how I desire You Lord. How my heart is aflame with passion for You. I am overwhelmed by your beauty and loving kindness. I am overcome with affection and adoration for You. I surrender all action. I give up on words and fall prostrate in reverent stillness.

I simply cannot express my abandonment to You with anything other than a tearful offering of my very self. All that I am and all that I have is yours.

Whatever shall come, and whatever may befall me, I will be yours forever and You will be mine. Nothing in this life or in death or in all eternity can ever separate us. Our spirits are entwined together and my whole being is ravished in the pleasure of experiencing You. You have taken up permanent residence in my soul, and You are continuously creating newness. You never stop making improvements to your home. I take great delight in all your work. I share every moment of life with You. I submit all my emotion to You. I exalt You with all that I am. With all of my strength I worship You alone, and have disregard for everything else. And I know with certainty – with complete assurance – that I will be one with You forever. I am yours and You are mine. Always. And nothing else matters.

Have you experienced the intense pleasure and peace of intimacy with Jesus?

DELIGHT

Take delight in the Lord, and he will give you the desires of your heart.

PSALM 37:4 NIV

My soul delights in You oh Lord! My heart explodes with pleasure. My whole being is exhilarated by your eternal majesty. By your unfailing love. Your wholesome goodness.

All of my soul rises to meet You and bows down in worship before You. Even the hairs on my arms rise up to honour You. My skin sings with exultation as I feel your pleasure pour over me.

You fill me with a sense of complete belonging. I rejoice in the certainty that I am yours forever and that nothing can separate me from You. I treasure a revelation deep in my soul – that You treasure me! I guard this knowledge in a vast steel vault within my heart. I place a blockade around this secret, held deep within my soul, that You delight in me.

Yes, You erupt with shouts of joy that I am yours! You are bursting with songs about me as You are overcome with pleasure in who I am to You. Your heart melts with emotion as You crown me, your beloved son.

And I am undone. I am overcome with humility and adoration that You should love me with such devotion. I shout back to You, and sob, and sing broken love songs of praise to You. I reciprocate your devotion with all my strength. All my being dances in the light of your love and desires to give back to You. And so we spin together wildly in a cycle of mutual delight. A pleasure-go-round of adoration and belonging. I am yours and You are mine – forever!

Oh how I long to stay in this perpetual, virtuous circle all the days of my existence. You place a crown of righteousness, authority, and freedom upon my head and I throw it down at your feet with abandon. All I have is from You and You are worthy of all I am and all I have. My soul delights in You. My heart exalts in your embrace. My being is flooded with assurance of your endless delight in me and your eternal promise to give me the desires of my heart. All I want is You.

Where does your soul find delight?

SATISFACTION

Jesus says, "I am the Gateway. To enter through me is to experience life, freedom, and satisfaction."

JOHN 10:9 TPT

I look around the room. I see a lot of cats. Domesticated animals that have no regard for their master. Preoccupied only with themselves and entirely unaware of the world around them. Ignorant of the love and power that provides their food and shelter. Disinterested in anything beyond their immediate appetite for nourishment and amusement. When threatened, they either run in fear or lash out, hissing with their claws.

And I observe that these cats are not so different from us.

The human tragedy is to live as civilized animals without any recognition of the God that brought us into being and sustains us. To eat and play; to labour and rest; to preen oneself and procreate, without embracing the spiritual life within. Without giving even so much as a fleeting thought to the existence, nature, and ways of God.

There are two people that look remarkably alike, but are worlds apart. One dwells exclusively in the physical world while the other is alive to the spiritual realm. One lives each day as though God doesn't exist, ruled by biology and materialism. The other strives to please God daily and yearns to know Him better. One seeks to satisfy the endless cravings of the body and mind, while the other pursues satisfaction in the knowledge and love of God.

Yes, there is nothing in the universe so tragic as a child of God running in a hamster wheel, ignorant of their creator, busily chasing appetites that only grow more insatiable with every taste that's taken.

The human spirit was created to desire and enjoy a deep, exhilarating, full satisfaction that can only be found in God. We are born with a need to receive deep, profound fulfilment from God.

Is your God-given hunger for satisfaction causing you to pursue Jesus or are you chasing worldly pleasures that can never satisfy?

FREEDOM

It's true that our freedom allows us to do anything, but that doesn't mean that everything we do is good for us. I'm free to do as I choose, but I choose to never be enslaved to anything.

1 CORINTHIANS 6:12 TPT

Oh Lord of righteousness, You rule with love. You alone are God, the omnipotent one, and You reign over all. You are God Almighty – the one from whom all power flows and is derived. Every creature only has the measure of power that You gave them. Yes, the all-loving, all-powerful God, rules the universe by giving power away. That's what Love does.

And when You empower, You give freedom – wholly and unreservedly – and in your integrity, You honour our choices and let us have our way. Even the angels were permitted to choose to rebel, and even now those demon angels still occupy their thrones within your government, abusing the delegated authority You lovingly gave them. Yes, we are all free – for good or for ill.

You created beings with the capacity and instinct to create and produce – to generate fruit in our own likeness, and to multiply for ourselves fruit that loves or fruit that poisons. Yes, we are all completely free to plant or uproot, to build or destroy, to give birth or to kill. History is our story of freedom, and the future is not yet written. It lies in the hearts and hands of your people. Of course You work through the affairs of mankind and You weave your purposes across all generations, but You will not violate our freedom. Instead,

You lovingly let us choose what to do with our today, our tomorrow, and our eternity – because You desire us to choose to be with You. Love cannot exist without freedom. Love cannot be compelled and must be chosen from a place of complete liberty – and so You made the bedrock of the universe one that is undetermined; one that supports freedom as well as randomness. And the crowning glory of your creation – the people that are the apple of your eye and were born from your breath – we decide what to do with all the power and authority You crowned us with. We have been given freedom and response-ability.

We have the ability to decide how to respond to God. We each decide what happens to our spirits, our bodies, our families, our neighbourhoods, and our planet. Yes, the earth and everything in it has been freely given to us to care for and to steward. Without freedom there is no responsibility, but with the great liberty God has given, we will one day give an account of how we used our precious freedom.

Are you proud of how you are using your God-given freedom? Will you choose to love God and to follow Him?

PROMISE

Every promise from the faithful God is pure and proves to be true. He is a wrap-around shield of protection for all his lovers who run to hide in him.

PROVERBS 30:5 TPT

I was sinking in deep, thick mud; consumed by despair, my every movement just hastened my demise. Escape was hopeless and I was lost to the dark quagmire that engulfed me. You pulled me up and placed me on a plateau of rock where I could rest; gave me mountain air so I could breathe; washed me down and cleaned out my wounds; strengthened my bones so I could stand again and see the view. You showed me an open field of golden grain, singing within your gentle breeze. You showed me a lush meadow of emerald as far as my eyes could see, well-watered by your ever-flowing stream of pure love. You told me it was mine; that You had carved it out and prepared it, and given it to me as a sign of your never-ending love for me. As a banner for all to see, for all eternity, that I am your adopted son and that You are my Good Father.

You suggested I make my home there; invited me to make the journey to travel there and take hold of it as my possession. So I left the security of my mountain cave and travelled over calamitous ridges; traversed a jagged precipice and navigated treacherous territories without fear because You were with me; because You burned your promise into my mind's eye. I persevered through every thicket and every dead-end path I wandered down, until I arrived at the spacious place that You had showed me. And I discovered that although I had arrived, the journey had not ended; that my struggle would continue as I fought to occupy more of the territory You had given me.

And so my life has become a journey of spreading out in the land of your endless promises and incrementally taking possession of what You have given me. Every day is a day of victory and battle within your land of rest and promise. All the promises of God are assured for me as I remain living in Christ Jesus, my promised land. I stretch out and explore the vast fields and valleys. I discover your power and goodness around every corner; your mercy under every tree. Yes, I stretch out and make the land mine. I overcome every obstacle and defeat every enemy that stands in the way. I settle the territory and place my name on it forever – for me and my children, and their children, and so on. Surely the goodness and love of my God will cover me and my descendants forever, across the galaxies of time, because your faithfulness never ends, and never fails. You have promised good for me and I will fight every day to take possession of your promises and enter the rest You have given me.

Will you dedicate yourself daily, to discovering, occupying and resting in the myriad of promises that you have in Jesus, our Promised One?

UNITY

Be completely humble and gentle; be patient, bearing with one another in love.
Make every effort to keep the unity of the Spirit through the bond of peace.
There is one body and one Spirit, just as you were called to one hope when you
were called; one Lord, one faith, one baptism; one God and Father of all,
who is over all and through all and in all.

EPHESIANS 4:2-6 NIV

Oh Lord, my spirit is squeezed in a vice; my heart is crushed by a heavy weight that I can't shift. Tears flow unrestrained and I have no words. I barely have breath to breathe under the burden of my brothers' suffering.

I cry out to You for justice for my black brothers and sisters. For mass repentance to rise from your family to heaven. For your people to kneel upon injustice with all their weight and ask for mercy. And for your mercy to come like a rushing wind. For your compassion to flow like honey, bringing reconciliation and healing to our land. For leaders to return to the foundations of our humanity; to face the truth staring at us when we look in the mirror – that all people are equal and endowed by You with unassailable rights to life, liberty, and the pursuit of happiness – and that we have transgressed these truths in a most egregious manner.

Oh Lord, it is time for equalization. It is time for your people to love ALL of their neighbours. It is time for your church to celebrate that every tribe and tongue will bow before the Lamb that was slain. It is time for all ethnic groups to join in one song of celebration and jubilation together – that the Lord God Omnipotent reigns with love for all his creation. It is time for unity. And my great conviction is this: When the church enters an unbroken, unfearful, and all-embracing unity, we will take the promised land in a way never before seen in history. Just as the twelve tribes of Israel had to boldly stack hands together and agree that God's promises were true for all of them; and just as they had to move together as one body to face opposition and take the promised land – so we now, your people of all ethnic groups around the world will stand together against injustice and agree that ALL the promises of God in Christ Jesus are "Yes and Amen" for ALL of creation; for ALL people.

Lord make us agents of unity that we might all grab hold of the great and powerful promises that await us in Jesus' mighty name; those promises that we have yet to see fulfilled – because we have yet to unite with our brothers and sisters.

Will you repent and weep and stand in unity with all your neighbours?

FAVOURITE

Things never discovered or heard of before, things beyond our ability to imagine – these are the many things God has in store for all his lovers.

1 CORINTHIANS 2:9 TPT

Oh Father, where would I be without You? Where would I run for comfort in times of trouble? Who would I look to for strength? How would it be possible for me to breathe under the burden of grief and sin and hopelessness? And what would I do with all my shame?

You saved my life and gave me a new future. You washed me clean and gave me new clothes to wear. You called me your child and showered me with generosity and love. Yes, You adopted me and gave me a new name; told me I was part of your family. You knelt down beside me and taught me the family business. You showed me your ways and how to follow them. You instructed me one-to-one, day by day, giving me guidance, encouragement, and comfort.

And then You let me in on an ancient secret – one written on your hands before the sun exploded into being... You whispered in my ear and told me, "You are my favourite".

And I cried, because I knew it was true. I had always felt your unmerited, special affection for me; your unique pleasure in who I am. And just as Joseph began to dream after receiving his multi-coloured coat – the proof of his father's favouritism – so my heart began to fly like never before. This secret knowledge drew me off my perch and opened up the sky to me. It released me from the mundane and the humdrum and pulled me into a life of exhilaration.

And then You added to the secret something so incredible that I am overcome with joy just thinking about it... You told me that every one of your children was your favourite, if only they would come to know it. You showed me that every child is uniquely loved and celebrated and favoured – all we need to do to enter this reality is to believe You when You tell us. Yes, You are the only Father capable of this universal, outlandish favouritism. And this knowledge is so beautiful, and so marvellous – that not only am I your favourite, but so are all my beloved brothers and sisters.

And this truth has changed me forever, and my heart soars with thanks for your unreasonable, unbridled affection for each of your children.

Did you realise that you are God's favourite?

HOLY

I have not learned wisdom, nor have I attained to the knowledge of the Holy One. Who has gone up to heaven and come down? Whose hands have gathered up the wind? Who has wrapped up the waters in a cloak? Who has established all the ends of the earth? What is his name, and what is the name of his son?

PROVERBS 30:3-4 NIV

There is no one like You, oh Lord... Nothing in all creation can match your beauty and greatness. Nothing can be compared with You or even placed on the same measuring scale. You are so much more and other-than everything else in the universe. You are so thoroughly and distinctly Yourself. So unique, that You are beyond comparison and beyond description. You stand alone like the sun within its galaxy. You rank on your own and are in your own league.

The substance of your being cannot be deciphered or understood; the building blocks of your person cannot be discerned or fathomed. You are like an alien language without any referenceable derivation and without translation. You exist in your triune oneness, in the essence of who You are and You are set apart from all else in existence. And You are who You are. You will be who You will be. Forever and unchanging.

While everything known to mankind is finite and measurable, You alone are infinite; nothing can even be put alongside You without shrinking into invisible dust. Your immenseness stretches beyond all limits. You are so preeminent and are so much greater than we will ever comprehend. You measure the universe with the span of your hand. Yes, the size of a subatomic quark is closer in stature to the sun than the entire universe is to your infinite grandeur and unsurpassed majesty. You alone are Holy – completely distinct and unique; the one and only who is without compare. You are beyond all apprehension and so of course it follows that your ways are not our ways. And I marvel in wonder at your unbounded love towards your creation. I rejoice in the infinite sea of who You are. I am awestruck that You made humanity in your image; placed your essence in the heart of mankind, giving us freedom with the potential to love and to hate, to forgive and judge, to create and destroy.

I worship in astonished amazement that You call us to join You in your exclusive holiness. You invite us to run away with You and hide within your cloak of glory forever. You woo us to separate ourselves from all things and to join our spirits with You alone – united in an eternal union of holiness. Yes, You alone are holy and somehow You bring us to where You are.

Is the Lord Jesus calling you to forsake all other affections to join Him in holy embrace?

HOPE

Even youths grow tired and weary, and young men stumble and fall; but those who hope in the Lord will renew their strength. They will soar on wings like eagles; they will run and not grow weary, they will walk and not be faint.

ISAIAH 40:30-31 NIV

I lift my eyes above the horizon to the forbidding mountains in the distance. I desperately need help and I wonder... Where will my help come from?

And I know immediately that however it may come, there is only one source of help: the Lord God Almighty, who made the heavens and the earth. He is my helper and my friend. The one who flung the stars into space and gave me breath. All my hope is in You, oh Lord.

In my mind and my body, I feel hopeless and empty. I feel weak and cast adrift. There are no rational reasons to be hopeful. All the signs around me are pointing to failure and disgrace.

But in the midst of the darkness in my soul, my spirit burns with a fire of hope. I have hope in the unfailing love of my King and in the unwavering faithfulness of my Heavenly Father. Hope that He will never let me be put to shame. Hope that He will work everything together for my benefit; that all my mistakes, all the injustices I have suffered, and all my misfortunes will be woven together into a blessing – packaged up just for me.

Yes, the Lord is my one and only Hope and Salvation. He is my Helper and is always at hand when I need Him. He is always watching over me and watching over His promises to ensure He keeps them. He will never let me down. Even when everything seems lost, my hope will burn brightly within the darkness of my disappointment and I will rise above all my troubles.

Yes, I will speak to my soul and fan the flames of hope. And hope in the Lord will fill my soul. Hope in the Lord will lift me high above the mountains that bar my way and cast shadows of doubt upon my days. Hope in the Lord will bring strength to my weary soul. Strength to wait a little longer, and strength to look attentively across the landscape, alert with anticipation for His salvation, which is sure to come.

Will you fan the flames of hope in the Lord and rise above your disappointment?

FAITH

Be brave. Be strong. Don't give up. Expect God to get here soon.

PSALM 31:24 MSG

I am in awe at the power of expectations...

Expectations are both cause and effect. What you search for, you will find. What you look for, you will see. From the Observer Effect in Physics to the impact of consumer expectations on the economy – our expectations are a chief cause of the future. Those same expectations are most often the effect of hope or fear. The Placebo Effect is another such phenomenon where a patient's expectation of recovery can cause an improvement in their condition. How extraordinary that the immaterial thoughts in our minds can so profoundly drive outcomes in the physical world.

And I marvel that our expectations are the fulcrum between hope and faith; they are the turning point at which the essence of faith is visible and where faith becomes a force, creating the future of our lives. Hope gives birth to faith and its first visible steps of life are positive expectations for today and tomorrow...

Oh Lord, I pray that You would work in the arena of my expectations.

That they would always be the product of hope and always be infused with your wisdom and truth. Thank you Lord that You have given me faith in your unfailing love. This is my most precious possession. This is my foundation and the scaffold on which my life is built.

Yes, the assurance of your love for me is like a building frame of steel girders on which all my expectations rest and stretch out – and this in turn shapes my life, for now and the future. The expectation of always seeing your goodness, of always receiving your mercy, of You always splitting the sea for me and making a way through the desert. These expectations mark out the height and width, the size and shape of the frame of my life. And they determine my future. Everything I have and anything of value that I will ever do, is built upon faith in You and the expectations that spring out of that faith like mighty guardrails. Yes, expectations are the real, steely substance of my faith – the spine on which the flesh of my life is formed. They give structure to my days and create strength beneath my actions.

What expectations are you building your life upon?

SUFFERING

Surely he took up our pain and bore our suffering... he was pierced for our transgressions, he was crushed for our iniquities; the punishment that brought us peace was on him, and by his wounds we are healed.

ISAIAH 53:4A-5 NIV

Oh my Jesus. My saviour. How I love You!

You sustain me and bring nourishment to my soul. You comfort me. You are my constant companion on lonely roads. You lift my eyes when I am down. You dry my tears. You cover me with your embrace. You share in my suffering, oh Lamb of God. You understand the depths of my pain and while You can't carry my burden, You carry me in your arms. You join me in my brokenness and fill me with your compassion. You sit with me in my silent grief. In my bitter sorrow, I cry on your shoulder. I lay my head upon your chest and wrap my arms around You. Your heartbeat quietens me. Your tears join with mine as You participate in my anguish and partake of my sadness. You lighten my load and help me catch my breath.

Where would I be without You? Every day I need your strength to stand. Your encouragement to smile. Your mercy to pull me through. You give me more than sympathy. You are more than a companion. You somehow take my place but without replacing me. You are somehow unified with me in my hardship, validating my unique experience, while also appropriating all my emotion onto yourself and into your being.

You absorb the intensity of my sobs, and hold the weight of my tears. You bring stillness to my soul. You are the Lamb that suffers all – taking upon yourself the pain of every atrocity and abuse – present, future and past. And I am bewildered by your capacity to swallow it all; overwhelmed at your commitment and attentiveness to absorb every drop of sorrow into your being.

And then I remember that You are the Lion and the Lamb; that You fiercely defend and protect your young; that You relentlessly pursue my healing and wholeness. Yes, within your sacrifice for all mankind is the ferocious rage and power of the Lion; and within the strength of your roar is the compassion of the Lamb. Oh my Jesus, I lay lifeless and still in your arms with exhausted thanks. I am drained of all emotion but am at peace. You comfort and restore me. You protect and renew me. Surely I will get through this, and You will bring newness of life to my weary bones. The Lion and the Lamb guard and empower my every step and I will hold onto You.

Will you let the Lord Jesus share in your suffering?

PATIENCE

I remain confident of this: I will see the goodness of the Lord in the land of the living. Wait for the Lord; be strong and take heart and wait for the Lord.

PSALM 27:13-14 NIV

My soul cries out to the black sky in the dull quiet of the night, How long Lord? How long until I see your deliverance? How long before I feel free again?

My troubles hem me in on every side, pressing against me. I have no room for manoeuvre. No chance to catch my breath.

How long must I wait, Father, for You to lead me into a spacious place again? My soul is weary of waiting. My mind is worn out with racing, and my heart is failing from pacing back and forth in the cage of my circumstances. Oh my Father, please make a way for me and don't delay any longer. I lack the strength to keep holding on. Please sustain me and revive me. Restore my soul and bring light back into my eyes. Breathe new life into me oh Lord...

I have no words left... and so I pause and listen. I hear only the rhythm of my breathing... feel only the thud of my heart in my chest. I look back up to the dark sky and notice that the moon has risen. The sign in the sky that although I am in darkness, the sun is still shining somewhere, and given time, will again shine on me.

And I know my Lord has not abandoned me. Even in my darkness on the desolate landscape of my troubles, there is evidence of His light, offering a promise that a new day will dawn.

And so I stare at the moon with quiet reverence. I meditate on its significance. On the sign, that the invisible sun can even be seen through the dead, abandoned dust of the moon. And I have hope that morning will come.

I remember your great faithfulness and your love that never fails. I draw strength from your promises. I depend on You alone, my provider. I will not give in to despair. I will wait for You, the one who makes me strong to stand, and gives me hope. Yes, I will wait for You to rise, with hope in my heart and with certainty that a new day will dawn soon enough. It won't be long before I again taste your goodness and find rest from my troubles.

Will you allow the Lord's unfailing love to give you strength to wait a little longer?

PERSEVERANCE

Let us throw off everything that hinders and the sin that so easily entangles.
And let us run with perseverance the race marked out for us, fixing our eyes on
Jesus, the pioneer and perfecter of faith. For the joy set before him he endured
the cross, scorning its shame, and sat down at the right hand of the throne of
God. Consider him who endured such opposition from sinners, so that you will
not grow weary and lose heart.

HEBREWS 12:1B-3 NIV

Father, where have You been when I called? Why are You silent as I cry? Why do You watch from afar as I am squeezed in the vice of life's pressures?

You are distant from me and I can't see your face. At night in my bed, I toss and turn and yearn for a glimpse of You. I plead with You for a dream to bring strength to my being and to lighten my load, but I awake feeling the same emptiness and weakness as when I laid down.

My first steps into the new day are heavy. My weary shoulders are slumped. My vision is clouded and my thinking is confused and muddy. There is too much to do. Too much depending on me. Too many battles to fight and too many arguments to be made.

I have no strength left. No will to carry on. I drop to my knees beside my bed and weep to You. I moan your name, Daddy. I can't face the day... I am hemmed in on every side and I can't stand it any longer... I need You. You are my very breath and I need your strength, your sustenance.

I take a deep breath and slow down. My whole being rests in You as I reduce my life to just simply breathing with You. I breathe in your comfort, your tender embrace. I breathe out and let go of my weariness, my inadequacy. I breathe in. I invite You into each of my crises. I am not alone. You are always with me. Sustaining my life. My roots are in You. Giving me strength, renewing my soul.

I know I have the strength for today. And I know that is all I ever need. Through each day, I will persevere. I will continue to stand and will endure every storm and I will never give up.

Who holds you steady through the storm?

INADEQUACY

But he said to me, "My grace is sufficient for you, for my power is made perfect in weakness." Therefore I will boast all the more gladly about my weaknesses, so that Christ's power may rest on me. That is why, for Christ's sake, I delight in weaknesses, in insults, in hardships, in persecutions, in difficulties. For when I am weak, then I am strong.

2 CORINTHIANS 12:9-10 NIV

Oh my Father, I lack the ability and the strength. I am simply not able to be the mother and father that my children need me to be... and my heart is breaking. Everywhere I look there is unfulfilled need. An empty space where their mother should be.

I am so unequal to the task. My understanding and wisdom is insufficient. My skills and talent are not enough. My thinking and empathy fall short. I don't have the language or the words. I don't have the patience or the time. My energy is sapped and all the force of my love can't stretch across the distance or fill the gap. I am drowning. I can't measure up. I am not enough, and my sense of inadequacy is overwhelming... oh Lord, help me! Please!

I sit silently in my weakness and I remember that I may be weak, but God is strong. I may be inadequate, but He is more than enough and His grace is sufficient for me.

And I give the burden of 'being enough' to God. I let go of the very idea or notion that I could ever be enough. I invite the Lord into the space of my inadequacy; to fill it with His all-sufficiency.

I lift the hearts of my precious children to You oh Lord and ask that You would be their comfort, their peace, their assurance; that they would know You as the lover of their souls; that your mercy and grace would cover over all my failures as a parent. Oh my Jesus, how desperately I need You! Please make up for my deficiencies and help me to meet their needs of body, mind, and spirit.

I meditate on the Lord's mighty power to save and to redeem, and I remember King David's mighty men. Weren't they all in debt to begin with? Weren't they a rabble of wounded, inadequate bankrupts who couldn't measure up to the world's demands? And didn't You make them into a fighting force like no other? Into super-humans who were more than enough? Who single-handedly overcame a whole army of enemies?

Oh Lord, please redeem my life. Turn my poverty into plenty, and my deficiency into strength. Oh Lord, may I rise up through your grace in your mighty power to overcome all that I lack.

Will you give the Lord your inadequacy today?

POWER

I pray that he would unveil within you the unlimited riches of his glory and favor until supernatural strength floods your innermost being with his divine might and explosive power. Then, by constantly using your faith, the life of Christ will be released deep inside you, and the resting place of his love will become the very source and root of your life. Then you will be empowered to discover what every holy one experiences – the great magnitude of the astonishing love of Christ in all its dimensions.

EPHESIANS 3:16-18 TPT

Where does the strength come from to stand in the face of overwhelming opposition? To weather the pain of grief and loss? Or to forgive the most egregious violations?

It comes from within – and such power is only available from one source.

As we receive power from God to comprehend how vast Jesus' love truly is for us, we also receive power for life.

When we become convinced – deep in our souls – of God's unlimited, unqualified, absolute love for us and of His delight in us as His favourite son or daughter, we are changed from the inside out.

We are emboldened. We are empowered with faith and perseverance to overcome the most insurmountable obstacles.

To know God's love, is to have power for life.
Power to navigate, to endure, and to thrive amidst any circumstances.

Yes, the power to stand in the face of adversity comes only from a revelation of God's unfailing love.

Oh that everyone, everywhere, would know this unworldly, unstoppable love that surpasses all understanding.

Have you received the power you need for life?

DISCIPLINE

He said, "My child, don't underestimate the value of the discipline and training of the Lord God, or get depressed when he has to correct you. For the Lord's training of your life is the evidence of his faithful love. And when he draws you to himself, it proves you are his delightful child." Fully embrace God's correction as part of your training, for he is doing what any loving father does for his children.

HEBREWS 12:5B-7A TPT

I used your mercy as a licence to transgress; I took your grace as a red carpet to walk over, and I wandered away from You. I marched in the opposite direction and trampled on your precepts. I crushed your choice words of affection under my clumsy feet as I ran after other pleasures. I blindly ran into thickets of thorns. I fell and broke my legs in a deep, dirty well where no one could find me. A dungeon of pain and shame where no one could hear me. I experienced discipline for my sin.

But You came looking for me. You sent search parties across the mountains. You dredged up the deepest sea. You wouldn't rest until I was safe in your arms again. You found me and renewed me. You healed me and forgave me and offered me even greater freedom than before.

I ran again, but this time, not with the strength of a man, but with the might of a horse. And as soon as I discovered my power, I blew You off. I ran away from your discipline. I raced through desert plains searching for water. I galloped over hilltops hunting for food. I couldn't find satisfaction anywhere and not a single tree gave me rest. I received discipline for my selfishness.

And all the while You were calling for me to return. Whispering to me words of your constant devotion. You were waiting for me, right where I left You. You embraced me and calmed my nerves; soothed my spirit. You trained my muscles and taught me how to work. You showed me a new way to channel my energy – to harness my power in worship. I took your yoke upon my neck and partnered with You. I learned the discipline of service and I developed new muscles of faithfulness from observing your example. Inwardly, I grew the power to be resolute in the light of your constant companionship. And then it got hard. The weather shifted and the landscape changed. My whole life was uphill. Every day I sailed against the wind. But You encouraged me. You told me that I was like a marathon runner in the last mile; like a weight-lifter, on my tenth repetition. And You cheered me on with the truth that the final exertion against this resistance would do me the most good. Would be the most beneficial to me. So I shouldered the weight in worship to You. I endured the discipline of hardship and so became a person of endurance. Yes, in your great love and faithfulness, You built me up with your discipline. Thank You Father.

Is the Lord showing You his love through discipline?
Are you submitting to it?

VICTORY

---

*For our struggle is not against flesh and blood, but against the rulers,
against the authorities, against the powers of this dark world and against
the spiritual forces of evil in the heavenly realms. Therefore put on the full
armour of God, so that when the day of evil comes, you may be able to stand
your ground, and after you have done everything, to stand.*

EPHESIANS 6:12-13 NIV

I was tired of persevering; tired of the fight. And I was done.

I grumbled and shouted my complaint to the Lord:
"Is it always going to be this hard? Is life always just going to be a
constant battle? I mean, will we ever win? Will we ever arrive at our
destination? Why does it have to be a constant struggle?"

And He answered me softly:
"Eric, my son, to fight is to win... To stand in the battle is victory!
The very act of continuing to fight, of continuing to stand in your
faith – that is victory! So keep standing! Keep fighting! To fight...
is to win!"

And this was just what I needed to hear! Your words brought
strength to my bones. Your encouragement straightened my spine.
And You brought joy to my heart with this truth!

Yes, I quickly shifted from feeling beaten down and worn out, to
feeling victorious! I was standing... and so I was victorious!

Yes, the joy of the Lord became my strength in my moment of
weakness and wavering. You gave me strength by calling me a victor.

And You turned my thoughts to Jesus. You drew my eyes back to
Him and away from my condition and my complaints. I considered
His victory. How He overcame through sacrifice. How He gave all
mankind the victory over sin, death, and the devil, through His
endurance of the most cruel and unjust punishment; through His
passion to carry on and to press through all that You gave Him to
do. And it was all for us.

My adolescent objections became tears of thanks and whimpers of
joyful appreciation. Yes, You put my feet on a rock and asked me to
stand – and that's what I'll do... through all weather. And that is my
victory in Jesus.

Have you come to know, deep in your heart, that simply staying in
the fight, is your victory?

RECKLESS

With your help I can advance against a troop; with my God I can scale a wall. As for God, his way is perfect: The Lord's word is flawless; he shields all who take refuge in him. For who is God besides the Lord? And who is the Rock except our God? It is God who arms me with strength, and keeps my way secure. He makes my feet like the feet of a deer; he causes me to stand on the heights. He trains my hands for battle; my arms can bend a bow of bronze.

PSALM 18:29-34 NIV

Lord of the ages. Master of the universe. I welcome You into my soul. I desire You with all my being. Come to me Lord and breathe into me your wisdom. Your peace. Breathe into me a humble spirit.

Make me an agent of your mercy on the earth. Give me a generous and compassionate heart that will always break for those in need. Give me a soul that will always stretch towards the widow, the orphan, and the destitute. Give me the means, the occasion, the inspiration, and the determination to go out of my way to help those I encounter on my path. Bring them to me Lord so I can be the arms and legs and hands of your mercy and compassion.

Give me boldness and prudence. Give me recklessness and wisdom. Give me your spirit of faith and revelation that I might follow wherever You lead. Anoint the eyes of my spirit so I will be transfixed with You and never lose sight of You. Oh Lord protect me from the world of distraction that besieges me. Shelter me within a vision of your unfailing love and your faithfulness that reaches to skies. Protect me within a clear picture of your eternal mercy and overwhelming goodness. May a vision of Jesus my saviour be a forcefield around me, and may I only see You. May I jealously pursue oneness with You all the days of my life.

And may I pull all those I love, and many others, into this incredible vision of You – the Lord God Almighty, the Omnipotent One – who reigns with love and mercy; who gives power and freedom to all creation; who has adopted us as His precious children; and who never fails to show compassion and devotion to his kids. You are so worthy of all our praise; so worthy of our very lives. Thank you Father, Saviour, Spirit. You have saved me and will shield me forever within a vision of You.

With You I can climb the highest mountain. I can scale the most forbidding wall. I can advance against an army of opposition. Nothing will intimidate me and nothing will stop me from pursuing You and your will. Yes, I can do all things through Jesus, who makes me strong. With Him I can overcome any challenge, and any obstacle.

Have you known the assurance and power of being recklessly abandoned to God alone?

ADVENTURE

---

*The one I love calls to me: "Arise, my dearest. Hurry, my darling.
Come away with me! I have come as you have asked to draw you to my
heart and lead you out. For now is the time, my beautiful one."*

SONG OF SONGS 2:10 TPT

Oh Jesus, my Lord, You are mighty! Mighty to save and mighty to rescue; more powerful than any other... and You are my Defender. You are my strong shield. You are my Deliverer – the one who scoops me up in times of danger and whisks me away.

You invite me on a journey of trust. You call my name and I come running. Oh how I love to hear You speak my name. You woo me with the sound of your voice. You romance me with your words, strong and softly spoken, and I will follow You anywhere. Not out of a sense of duty but because I want to be with You; because my heart's delight is being with You, and the greatest exhilaration to be found in all of life, is in You.

No, I will never stray from You. I long to be with You, and wherever You are, that's where I will be too. Trust and obedience fade in the rear-view mirror. They cease to be a factor. Uncertainty and fear are no longer part of my experience – they fail to even make an appearance on the horizon.

Yes, You lead me on an adventure; a voyage of discovery.

Every day I explore new depths of your being; unearth new treasures of your ways; pioneer new pathways of worship. Yes, I find new words and actions to show You my love and to give You my all; new avenues to your throne of grace. The territory of your goodness stretches beyond the horizon; the land of our adventure is endless and my appetite to learn from You is insatiable.

As we travel together, I also find myself. Yes, throughout our journey, my identity is formed and solidified. You shape me and mould me anew. You repair my broken places and soften my rough edges. You give me a laser sharp mind and make my heart like the clouds. A gentle breeze of compassion moves my heart; just a whisper of your wisdom shifts my mind into gear. All of my being is alert to You, tuned to You, in constant desire and adoration of You.

You are my life's adventure. You are my song, and I will sing with You and dance and skip along new paths of your love forever.

Is Jesus inviting you on an adventure to discover new life in Him?

OFFERING

Ascribe to the Lord, all you families of nations, ascribe to the Lord glory and strength. Ascribe to the Lord the glory due his name; bring an offering and come into his courts. Worship the Lord in the splendor of his holiness; tremble before him, all the earth. Say among the nations, "The Lord reigns."

PSALM 96:7-10A NIV

Oh my precious Jesus. There isn't space in my heart for all the praise I have for You. For all the love that continually explodes and springs from my spirit. I can't contain my thanks and praise!

The inexpressible joy of being with You – of simply basking in your glorious presence – bursts out of my throat and mouth with shouts of celebration. My whole being participates in a unified proclamation of your holy name; my spirit and body cry out in unison with noisy, exuberant worship! With a standing, dancing ovation of appreciation and adoration – all that is in me is united in unanimous agreement that You alone are to be glorified and exalted over all the earth. Yes, my heartbeat heralds applause for You. My breath endlessly calls out your name. My arms are palm branches waving in tribute to your Majesty. My hands are like birds flying on the wind with unbounded expressions of praise. My legs are cheetahs running after You; my feet like salmon skipping upstream in your ever-flowing love. My skin rejoices in your glorious light and I can't get enough of You. I can't shout enough or sing enough or dance enough. My very life is not expression enough to make an appropriate response to your greatness. You are so worthy of acclamation and so worthy of adoration that even when the whole of the universe dances together in abandoned worship, it is insufficient. It is paltry next to all that You deserve. So who am I to hold back? Who am I to keep quiet? I simply can't do anything other than spend all my strength on praising You. It is You that I live for, my King! You that I long for! You that I desire to see hallowed with fame, lavished with an outpouring of love, and lauded for who You are. Yes, I hear the mountains praising You. The rocks and the trees are screaming in agreement; the oceans and rivers roar their approval; even the grass and the insects pay homage to You. You alone are God and worthy of all creation's worship.

And yet those You stamped your image on; the crowning glory of your creation that You put your breath within; the ones that are called by your name; they turn their back on You. They stay quiet and ignore your wholesome goodness. Deny your fiery presence. And it is an afront to the stars. A mystery to the moon. All of creation shouts your name as the only appropriate response to your Holiness. And I will join in their dance and their song forever, in a universal offering to You. All that I am is yours, and though small, it is all that I have to offer. I give You my life with delight and without reservation.

What can you bring today as your offering to the King of the universe?

PERMANENCE

For I am convinced that neither death nor life, neither angels nor demons,
neither the present nor the future, nor any powers, neither height nor depth,
nor anything else in all creation, will be able to separate us from the love of
God that is in Christ Jesus our Lord.

ROMANS 8:38-39 NIV

You made me to last forever. My heart, my soul, my love, my relationships. You created them for eternity.

The flowers of the field are beautiful. They're exquisite in their delicate detail but they're gone in a season. They wither and perish. They disappear without a trace. Yes, the world has a lot to offer – many attractions to draw us and to delight in – but it will all pass away with time. Even mighty cliffs will crumble under the waves of your glory and mountains will be submerged within your never-ending love.

But your people will live with You for all eternity. We will experience the infinite bliss of union with You and unity with our brothers and sisters, forever. The intimacy, joy, worship, devotion, and delight will be permanent. Our pleasure in your goodness and our satisfaction in your victory will be eternal. And it will all be enveloped by your infinite love.

Yes, the things of this world – the battles and the joys – will be superseded by your eternal kingdom of truth and love. Everything around us – all that we can see – is temporary, but your invisible kingdom is everlasting. You... me... and all that we are together, with all the people of God... we... are permanent. Our togetherness is timeless and our mutual joy and adoration will be unceasing.

You fill my heart to overflowing with anticipation. You exhilarate my soul with the thought of our eternal dance. I am deeply fulfilled with the assurance that I will worship in your embrace with unbroken, unending, perfect praise, forever.

And I will still never be able to praise You enough.

Will you invite the Lord to thrill you with the permanence of His embrace?

THANKS AND ACKNOWLEDGEMENTS

For reviewing and giving honest feedback
Rolf Sandor, Rich di Castiglione, Tiffany Buhler, Ann Sandor

For book design
Joseph Paul
www.josephpaul.co.uk

For cover photography
Elia Pellegrini